LITERATURE ACTIVITIES
FOR
YOUNG CHILDREN

Written by Dianna Sullivan
Illustrated by Nedra L. Pence

Art Projects and Skill Building Activities

for

CHILDREN'S POETRY

selected from

Read-Aloud Rhymes for the Very Young selected by Jack Prelutsky (Knopf, 1986)

You Read to Me, I'll Read to You by John Ciardi (Harper & Row, 1962)

all the small poems by Valerie Worth (Farrar, 1987)

The Sky Is Full of Song edited by Lee Bennett Hopkins (Harper & Row, 1983)

Chicken Soup with Rice by Maurice Sendak (Scholastic, 1962)

A Child's Garden of Verses by Robert Louis Stevenson (Chronicle, 1989)

Teacher Created Materials
P.O. Box 1214
Huntington Beach, CA 92647
©1991 *Teacher Created Materials, Inc.*
Made in U.S.A.

ISBN 1–55734–298–9

Table of Contents

Note: The page number next to the title indicates the page on which the poem can be found in the resource given.

Extension Ideas

Selecting a Poem

Choose poems that:
1. contain language children will understand
2. reflect children's interests
3. include childhood experiences
4. exhibit a beauty of language
5. are timeless in subject matter

Teaching a Poem

1. Give children background information about the poem.

2. Set the stage for the poem by showing pictures and items that enhance the topic or setting of the poem.

3. Read the poem to the class with enthusiasm, feeling, correct intonations, and clarity.

4. Discuss the poem with the class. Talk about characters, setting, events, descriptive words, moods, content, author's purpose, and unfamiliar words.

5. Reread the poem while the children follow the words silently in their books. The children may whisper the words as the teacher recites the poem.

Extended Teaching Ideas for Poems

1. Children can guess from the title and the picture what the poem is about.

2. Choral Reading:
   - The whole class reads the poem together silently, then aloud.
   - Let girls take the first stanza and the boys the second. Reread the poem, reversing the order.
   - Divide the children into 2, 3, or 4 groups. Each group reads one stanza in unison.
   - One child reads a line or more solo; the class reads the stanza.
   - Choose several good readers to read a stanza aloud.

3. Children can explore the pictures surrounding a poem, then relate their own experiences (things they see, hear, taste, smell, touch).

4. Have children read aloud parts of a poem. For example, have them choose:
   - the funniest parts
   - descriptive words for a character, place, or thing
   - mood words

5. Draw pictures illustrating the incidents or stanzas of a poem.

6. Copy words, lines, stanzas, or the whole poem from the board onto paper.

Extension Ideas *(cont.)*

7. Have children make a display of physical objects mentioned in a poem.

8. Class may interpret the actions of a poem in pantomime. Dramatize parts or the whole poem or act out poems with finger plays.

9. Children may memorize a poem and recite the poem to the teacher, in front of a small group, or in front of the class. Offer stickers or small trinkets as rewards for poem memorization!

10. Encourage children to learn about authors/illustrators of poems. Write a group story about the author or illustrator.

11. Recite or list rhyming words in the poem for fun skill-building.

12. Have the children think of questions they would like to ask the main character. Questions can be asked verbally, listed on paper, or listed on the board.

13. Collect poems. Have children draw pictures depicting the poems. Bind child-illustrated poems into a classroom book. Place the book in the library corner for everyone to enjoy.

14. Make a mural of the poem depicting the characters, scenes, and mood(s) of the poem.

15. Choose a poem and glue it onto construction paper. Have the children illustrate the poem. Hang the poster on a wall for all to enjoy.

16. Have the children invent their own word pictures (similes). For example, suggest ''as quick as bunnies'', ''as red as apples'', or ''as scary as _____.''

17. Children write their own free verse poems in a ready-made framework. Use for example:

    I wish I could _____.
    I wish I were _____.
    Happiness is _____.

18. Read and write poems depicting the seasons or holidays. Collect them into your own holiday or season booklet.

19. Compare one poem with another.

20. With the help of the music teacher, have the children invent music for poems (or, poems for music!).

Footnote

1. Color and cut out shoe.

2. Glue to tagboard (laminate if desired).

3. Punch holes and use a shoelace to lace the shoe.

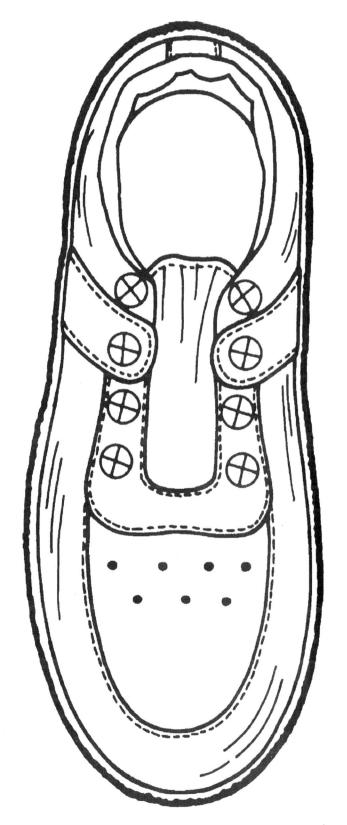

Name _____

The Little Turtle

the pictures. Tape a craft stick behind each circle to make puppets.

and

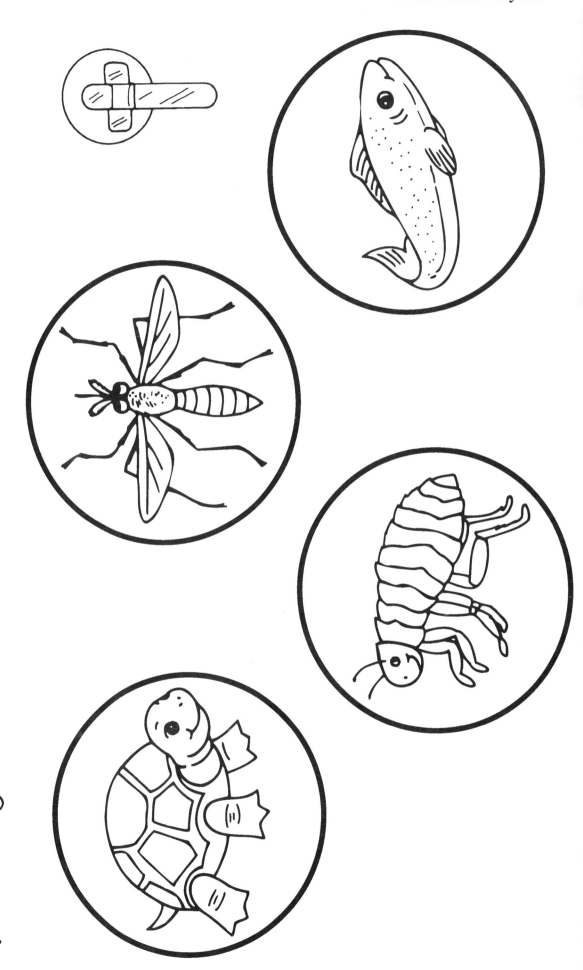

Name_____

The Frog on the Log

 the words on the frog.

frog	tree	flash
log	scree	splash

1. _____

2. _____ 3. _____

4. _____ 5. _____

6. _____

Mice

 a line to help the mouse get through the house. Color the picture.

Chums

 , , the puzzle pieces to make a dog picture.

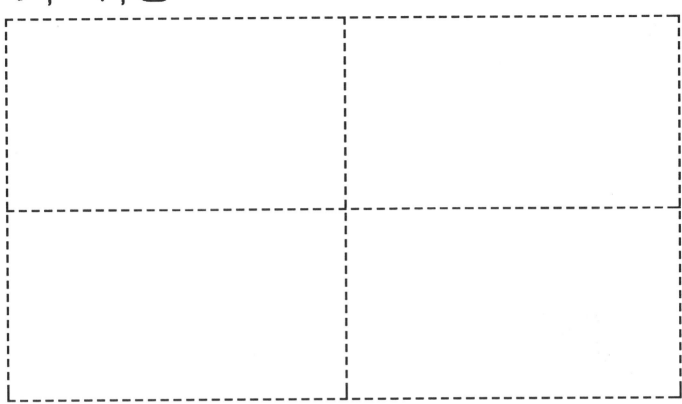

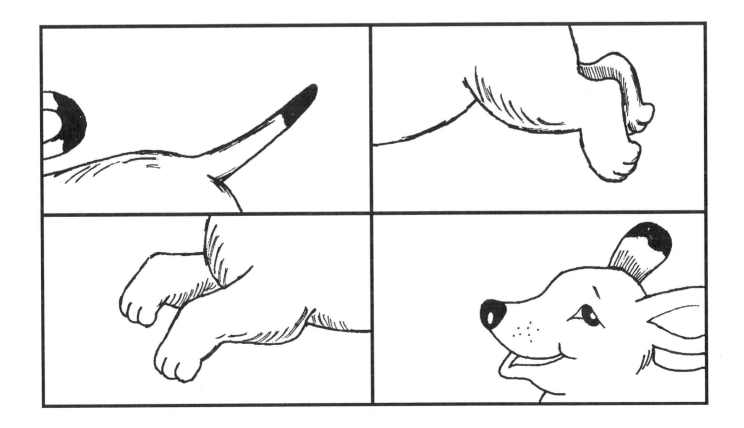

Fish

 , the pictures in the correct column.

Fish	Not Fish

Good Morning

, , the animal sounds to the animals.

4. "cheep, cheep"	1. "quack, quack"
2. "squeak, squeak"	3. "bow-wow-wow"

Name_____

Mix a Pancake

 , , the pictures in 1–2–3 order.

1. Mix and stir.	2. Fry and toss.	3. Butter and syrup.

Name_____

Teddy Bear, Teddy Bear

 , , the pictures in order.

1
2
3
4

3. Turn out the light.

1. Go upstairs.

4. Say "good night."

2. Say your prayers.

The Squirrel

Make ten copies of the squirrel and nut on brown construction paper. Cut out the pieces. Write a different number from 1-10 on each squirrel. Draw a different set of dots from 1-10 on each nut. Direct the child to match the numbers on the squirrels to the correct set of dots on the nuts (see example at right).

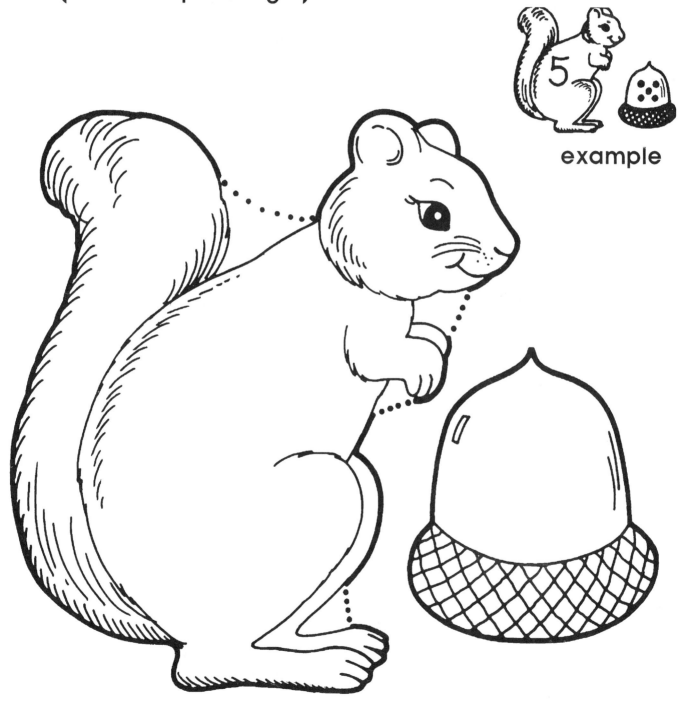

example

Raindrops

Find the answer. the picture.

If raindrops fell as big as you,
what would you do?

a 1

d 2

i 5

h 4

e 3

n 6

r 7

u 8

___ ___ ___   ___ ___ ___
7   8   6   1   6   2

___ ___ ___ ___!
4   5   2   3

Ants

 , , the pictures where they belong.

green	yellow
orange	red

red	yellow	green	orange

Name _____

The Star

✏️ , ✂️ , 🧴GLUE the stars that come next.

Open House

 each picture to its word name.

| 1. bird | 2. squirrel | 3. bear cub |

| 4. porcupine | 5. tree toad | 6. katydid |

Name_____

Sometimes

Name_____

Somersaults

 the picture.

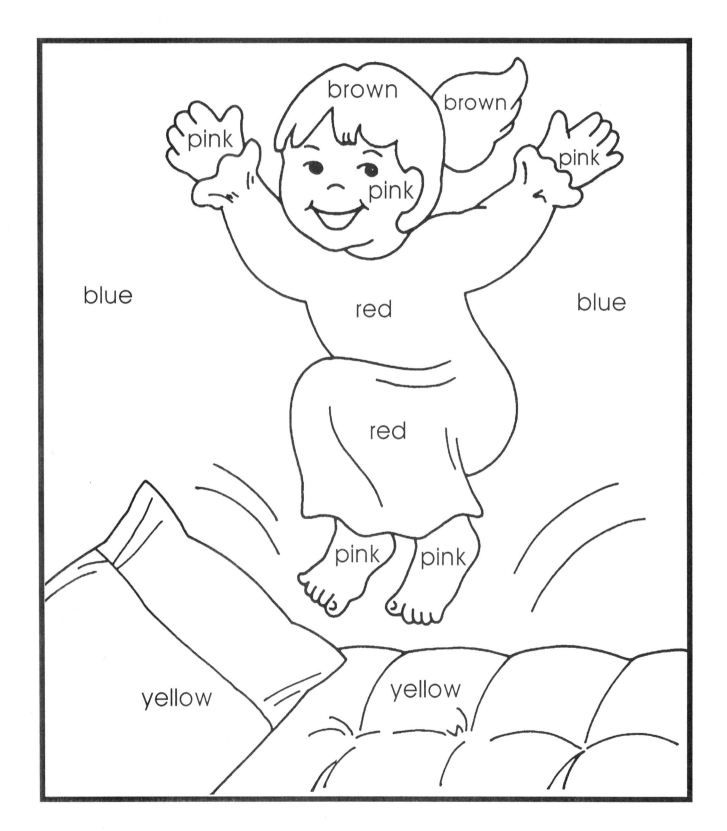

Name_____

You Read to Me, I'll Read to You

About the Teeth of Sharks

Make as many copies of the shark, below, as needed.

Cut rectangular pieces from wallpaper scraps. Glue one wallpaper rectangle to the shark's front half and a like wallpaper rectangle to the shark's back half. Cut out and laminate shark halves. Direct the child to match like wallpaper patterns on the shark halves to make whole sharks.

I Wouldn't

   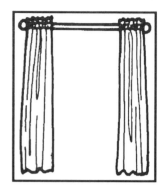

1. Color objects above.

2. Color the objects in the picture below the same as above.

What Night Would It Be?

 all the things in the poem.

About Jimmy James

Copy the tigers, below, five times; color and cut out. Label each tiger with a different number name from one to ten. Direct the child to sequence the number words in one to ten order.

Extension: Two children may play this game together. Place all the tigers face up in a pile. The first player chooses a tiger. The other child must find the *before* or *after* number word from the pile.

Name_____   *You Read to Me, I'll Read to You*

The Wise Hen

Trace the raindrops. the picture. the words.

Sometimes I Feel This Way

1. Color and cut out the pieces on this page.

2. Cut the two dotted lines on the girl's hair.

3. Push the strip through the back.

Sometimes I Feel This Way (cont.)

1. Color and cut out the pieces on this page.

2. Cut the two dotted lines on the boy's hair.

3. Push the strip through the back.

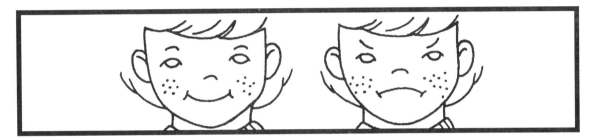

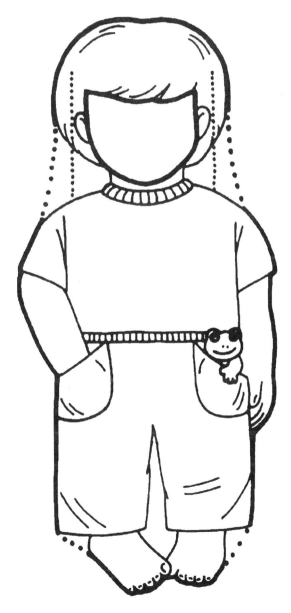

The Lighthouse-Keeper's White Mouse

1. Color and cut out the pieces on pages 28 and 29.

2. Cut out the space on the mouse's body.

3. Attach the wheel behind the mouse with a paper fastener through holes A and B (see diagram).

Have the child turn the wheel as he/she retells the poem.

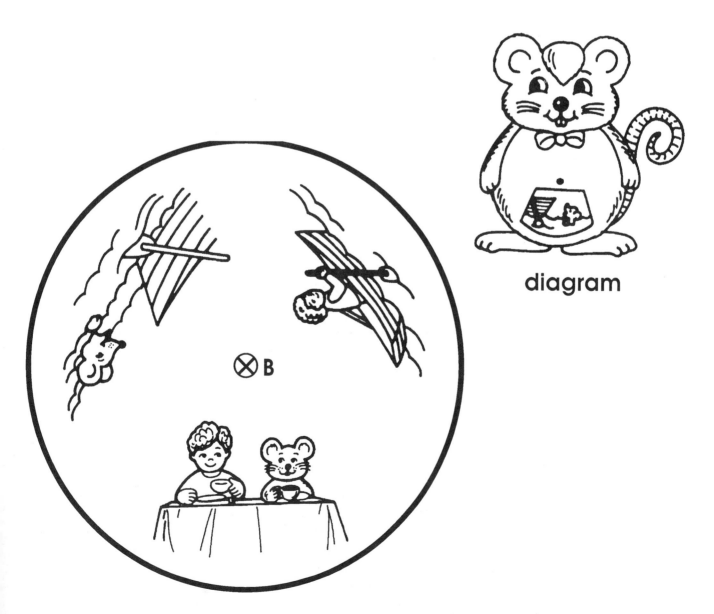

diagram

The Lighthouse-Keeper's White Mouse *(cont.)*

⊗ A

cut out

Name_____

A Warning About Bears...

More About Bears...
Still More About Bears...
Last Word About Bears...

Copy the bears, below, thirteen times; color and cut out. Print a capital letter on the front of the bear and print its corresponding lower case letter on the back of the bear. Tell the child to sequence the bears in A-B-C order, using upper or lower case letters.

What Did You Learn at the Zoo?

Read the word. the pictures.

orange

monkey

brown

kangaroo

brown and orange

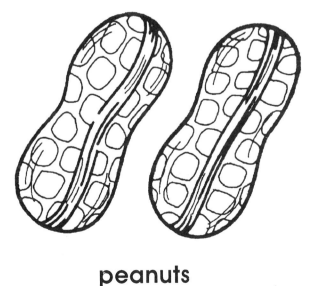

peanuts

yellow and green

bottle of lemon-and-lime

Name_____

Tell Him To Go Home

1. Color and cut out the pieces on pages 32 and 33.

2. Glue around side and bottom edges of pocket (this page).

3. Glue pocket to boy.

4. Store cards in pocket in story order.

diagram

Tell Him To Go Home *(cont.)*

pocket

The Bird-Brain Song

Copy the store pattern, below, and the cents cards on page 35. Color, cut out, and laminate. Place a pile of real or toy pennies beside the store. Shuffle the cents cards and place them face down in a pile. Direct the child to draw the top card, read the amount and count that many pennies. Have the child put the pennies back in the pile, draw another card, and repeat the process.

The Bird-Brain Song *(cont.)*

A Short Checklist of Things To Think About Before Being Born

 a line connecting the number to the picture.

3. How many brothers and sisters will you have?

1. Pick a father and mother.

2. Decide if you'll be a boy or a girl.

Cow

a line connecting the A-B-C dots. Color the picture.

Jewels

 the jewel on the left.

 the jewel on the right.

 the jewel in the middle.

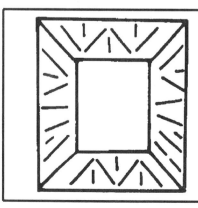  

38

Name_____

Marbles

 , , the marble that comes next.

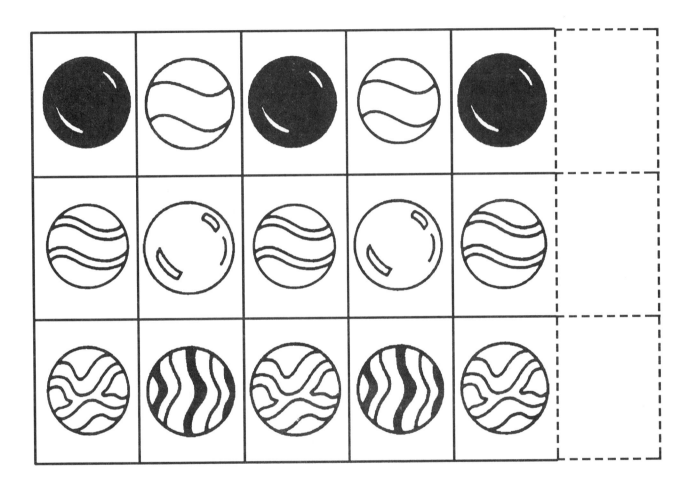

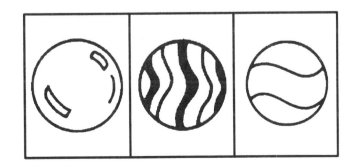

Duck

 , , the pieces in order onto construction paper to make a duck picture.

Frog

 and  the "circle spots" on top of the correct number on the frog.

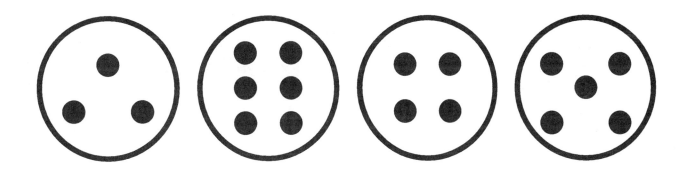

Pebbles

 , , the pieces where they belong.

Kitten

1. Color and cut out the pieces on pages 43 and 44.

2. Glue the "flaps" below to the tops of Tabs A-D.

3. Bend at dashed lines and open.

Diagram

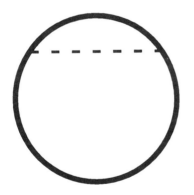

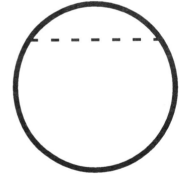

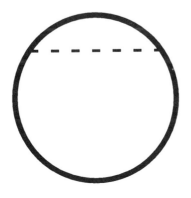

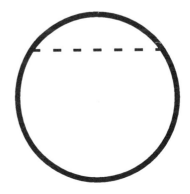

Kitten *(cont.)*

Tab A

Tab B

Tab C

Tab D

Flamingo

 the pictures.

 and the flamingos onto the correct ovals.

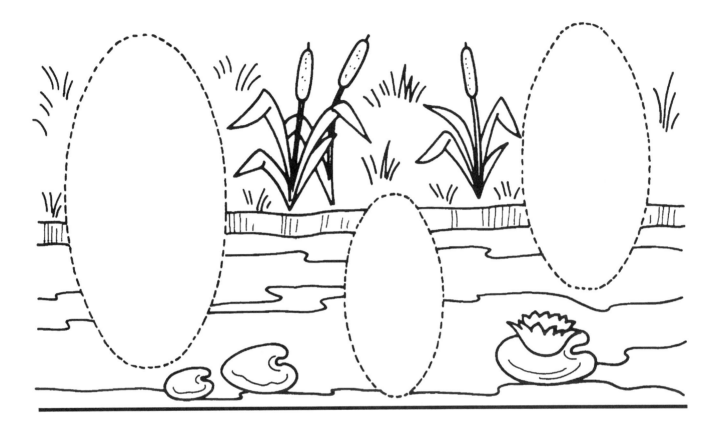

all the small poems

Mosquito

 the pieces onto a piece of construction paper to make a mosquito picture.

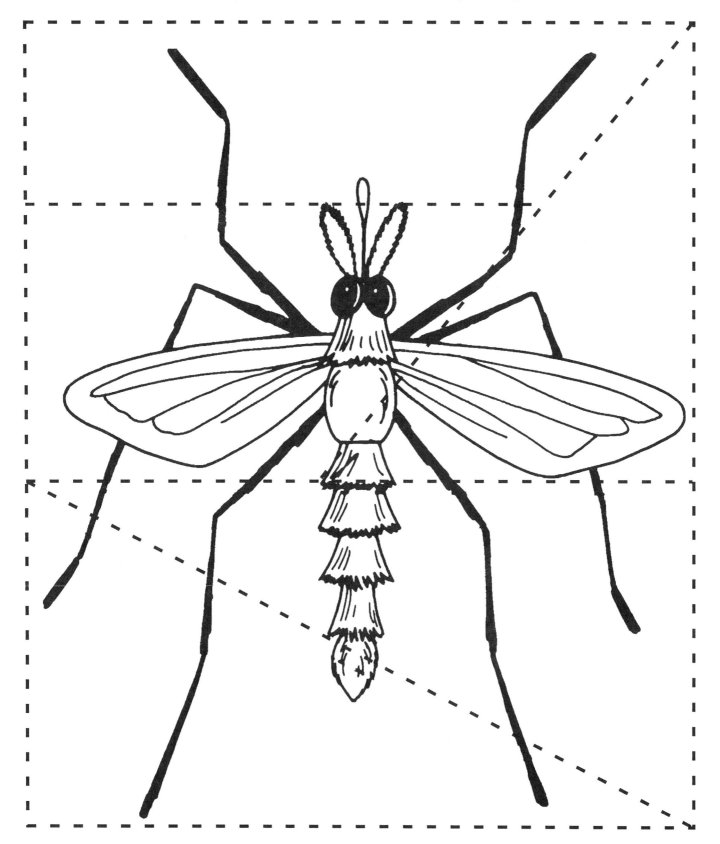

Sea Lions

and the pages. Staple the book together.

Sea Lions

Name_____

1 Sea lions nudge each other.

2 SPLASH! Sea lions fall into the water.

3 Sea lions swim in circles.

4 SNORT! SNORT! Sea lions make snorting sounds.

5 Sea lions slap their flippers.

Name_____

all the small poems

Pumpkin

 the pictures in order.

1	**2**
Cut a lid in the top of the pumpkin.	Scoop out the seeds.
3	**4**
Carve a face in the pumpkin.	Light a candle in the pumpkin.

48

Turtle

1. Color and cut out the pieces on pages 49 and 50.

2. Shell: Overlap line A on top of Tab A and glue. Glue or staple the shell onto the turtle's body (see diagram on page 50).

Turtle *(cont.)*

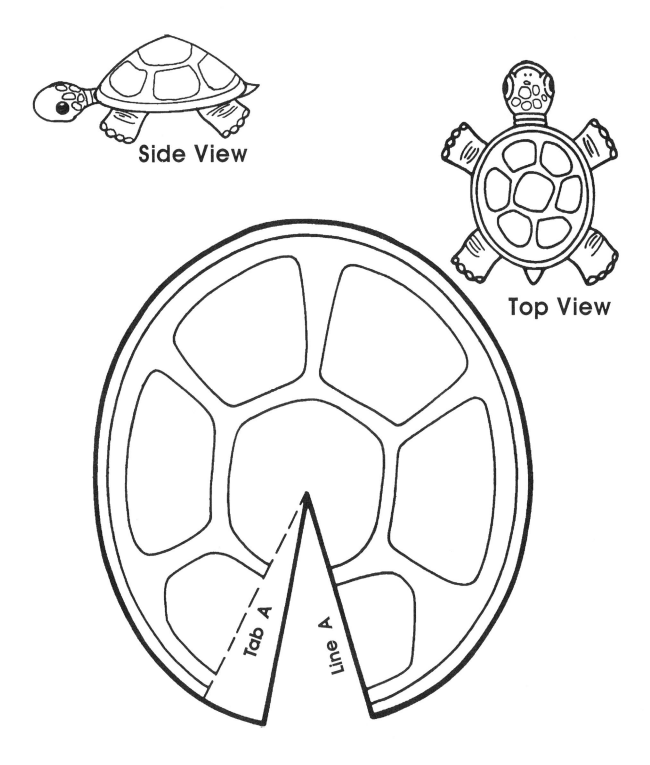

Side View

Top View

Tab A

Line A

Name_____

Sweets

 the words.  the pictures.

peppermint

strawberry

licorice

time

Giraffe

 , , the pictures in order.

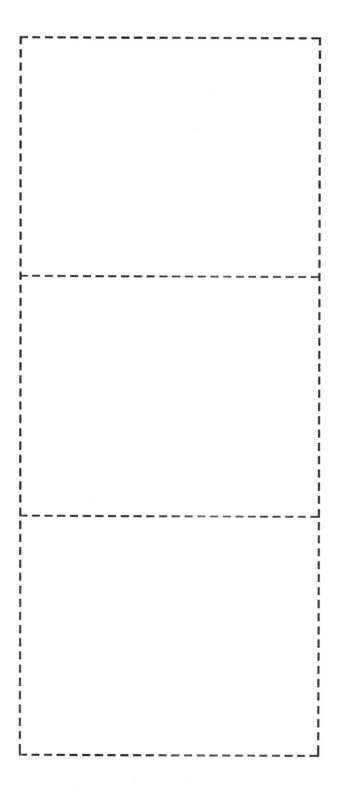

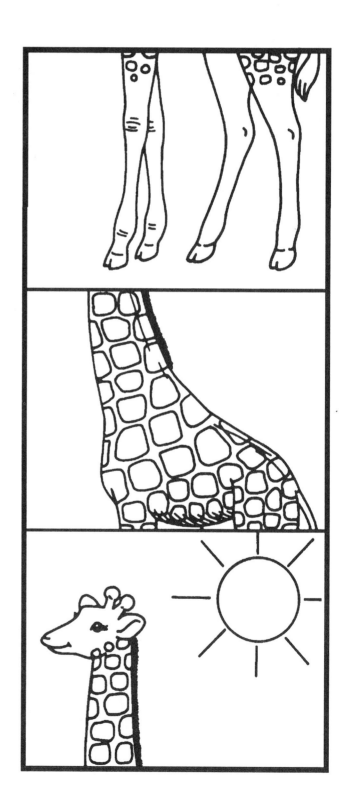

New Sounds

Circle and the pictures in the row that match the picture in the box.

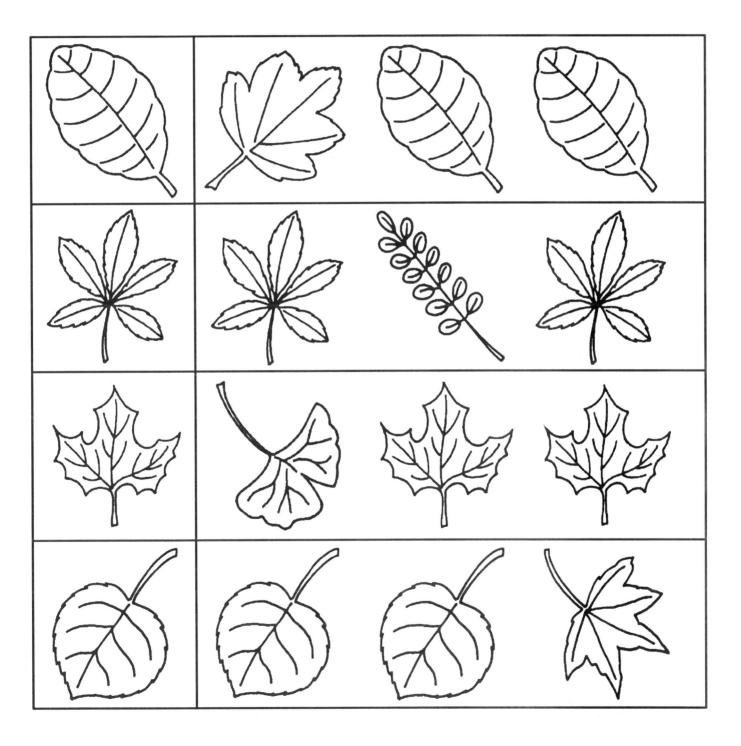

Name_____

The Pumpkin Tide

1. Color and cut out the pieces on pages 54 and 55.

2. Cut out the space on the pumpkin, below.

3. Fasten the wheel behind the pumpkin with a paper fastener through holes A and B. Turn the wheel to make different faces.

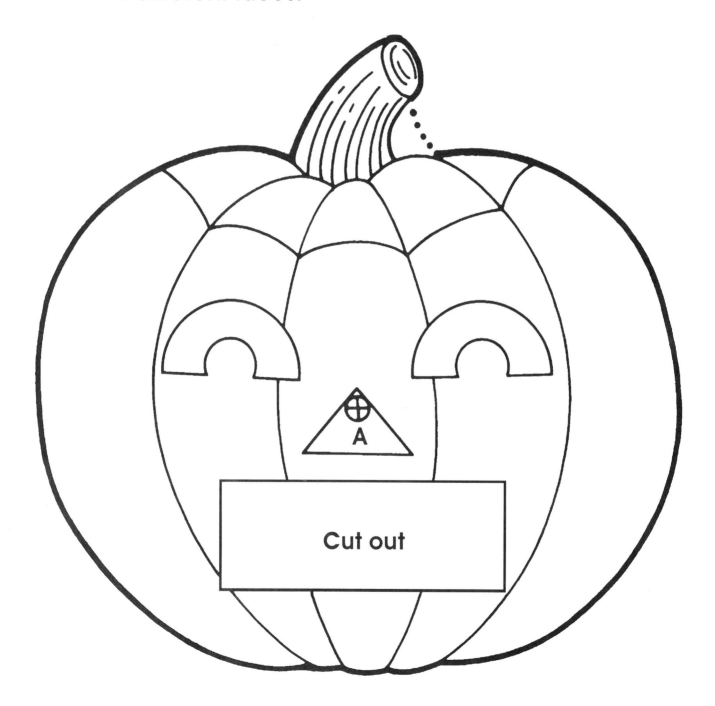

Name_____

The Pumpkin Tide *(cont.)*

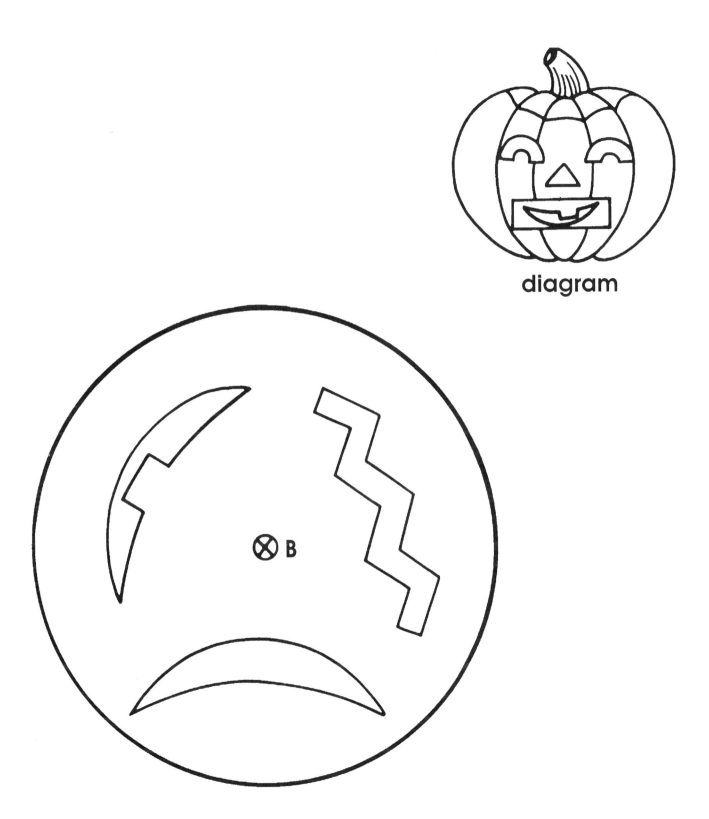

diagram

Thanksgiving

 a line to match the turkeys that are the same size.

The Day After Christmas

 a line matching the like wrappings. Color.

January

1. Color and cut out the pieces on pages 58 and 59.

2. Punch out holes A-D.

3. With string, connect the girl's head to her upper body. (Holes A and B), and her upper body to her lower body (holes C and D). See the diagram at left.

diagram

January *(cont.)*

Name_____

February Twilight

✏ by number.

1-red 2-yellow 3-pink 4-green 5-blue

60

Name_____

Tommy

 the pictures in order.

1	**2**
3	**4**

2. Water the plant.

1. Plant a seed.

4. The plant is growing!

3. Care for the plant.

April

Count the raindrops. Write the number in the box. Color.

How many raindrops?

Name_____

The Shadow Tree

 a line from the object to the shadow. the picture.

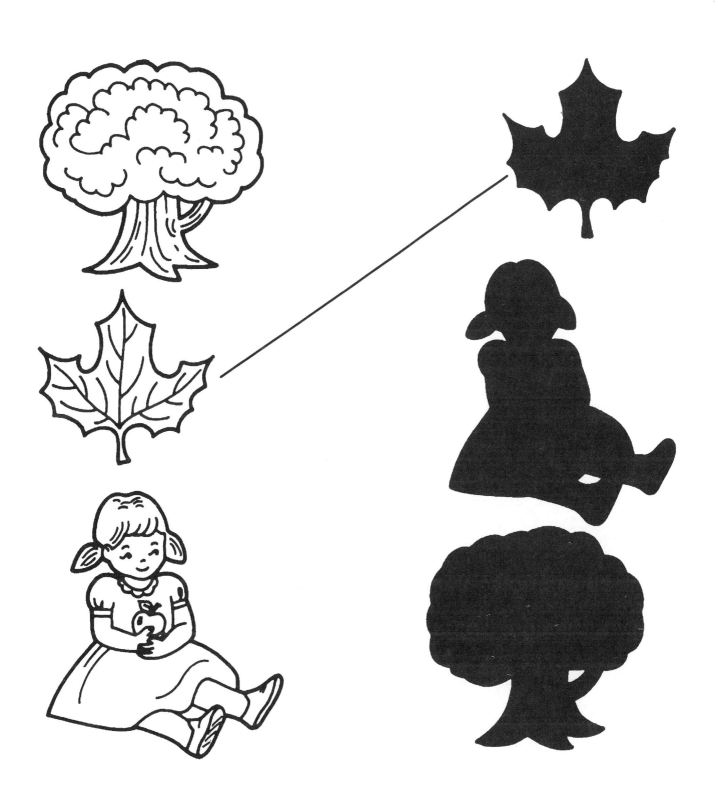

63

Down on My Tummy

Match the like seashells. Color.

The Sky Is Full of Song

Sitting in the Sand

 and   on the heavy lines.

cut

Sitting in the Sand *(cont.)*

 and ✂️ on the heavy lines.

cut

Name_____ *Chicken Soup with Rice*

January

Read the word. the picture.

red   blue   yellow   green

     67   *#298 Literature Activities for Young Children*

February

1. **Color and cut** out the pieces on pages 68 and 69.

2. **Glue the top** of the Snowman to Tab A (page 69).

3. **Arms:** Fold Tabs B and C downward. Attach them to the snowman's body behind his shoulders (see diagram).

diagram

68

February *(cont.)*

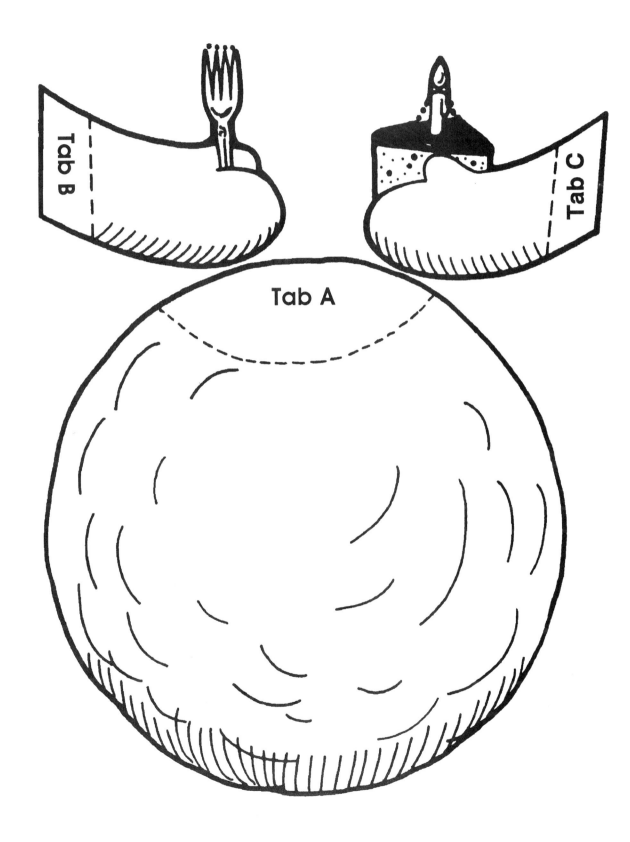

Tab B

Tab C

Tab A

Name_____

February

, , the pictures in order.

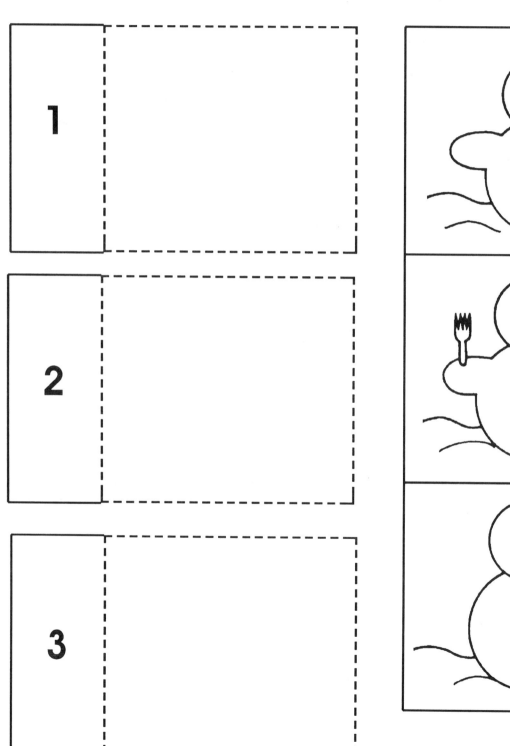

| 1 |
| 2 |
| 3 |

March

a line from the wind to the door.

April

 a line from the boy to Spain.

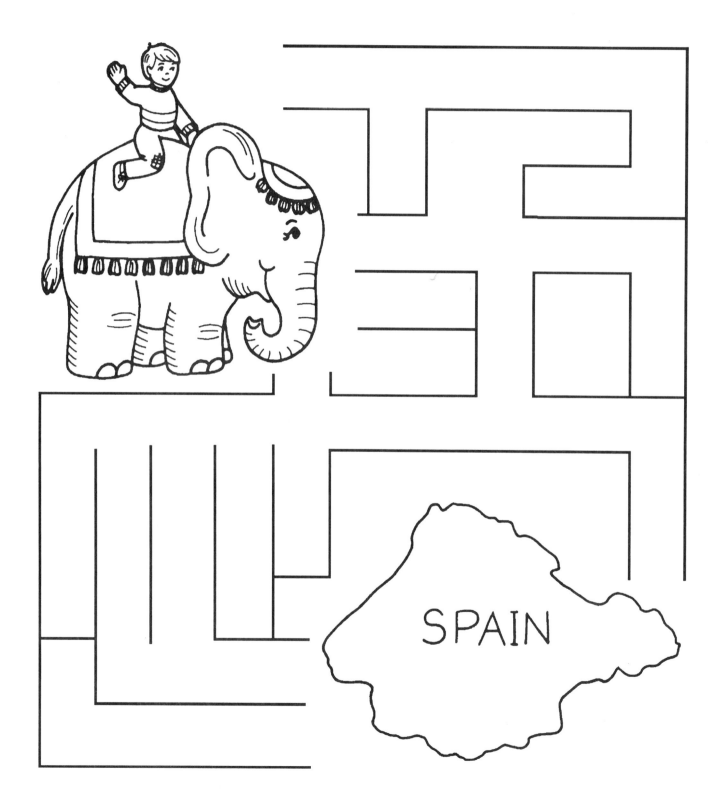

SPAIN

Name_____

May

Copy the bird and her nest 10 times on white construction paper; color and cut out. Label each bird with a number from 1-10. Draw sets of dots from 1-10 on the nests. Direct the child to match the numbers on the birds to the sets on the nests.

diagram

May

, the puzzle pieces to make a bird picture.

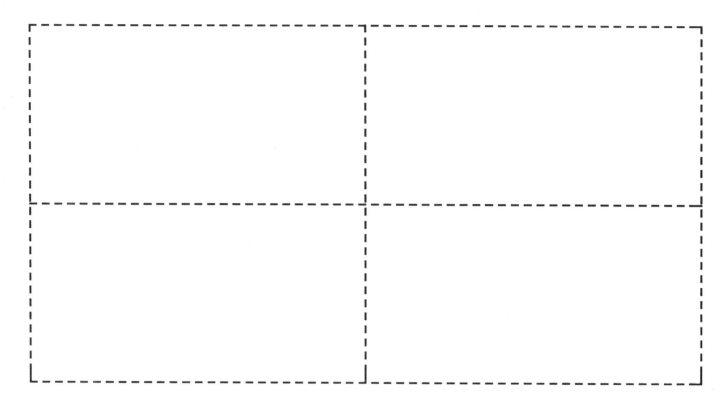

June

and ✂ out the flower pieces. Match the pieces to make three flowers. Glue the flowers onto green paper.

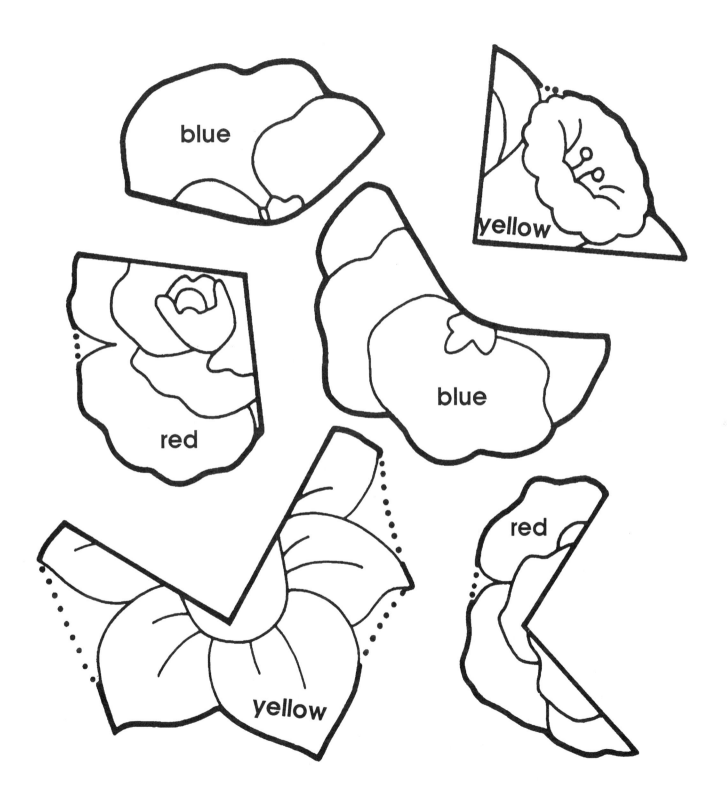

Name _____

July

✂ and 🍶 the pieces onto blue construction paper. Color.

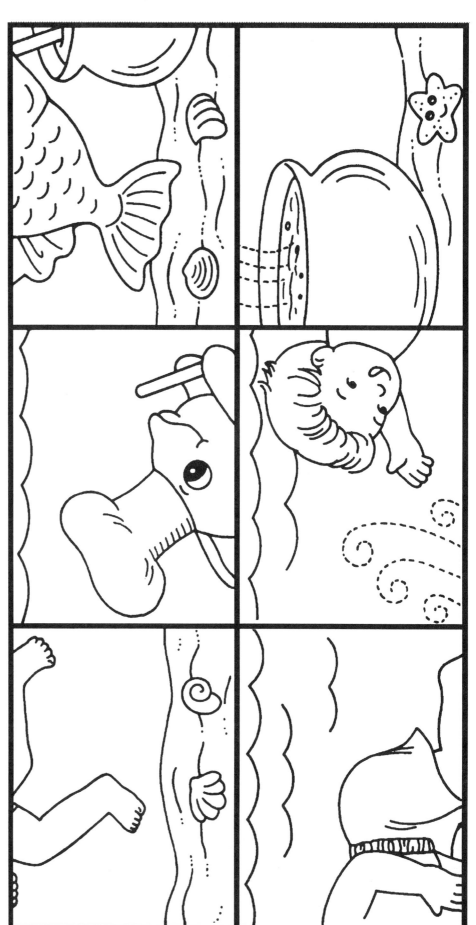

Chicken Soup with Rice

August

Read the sentences below. the spaces the correct colors.

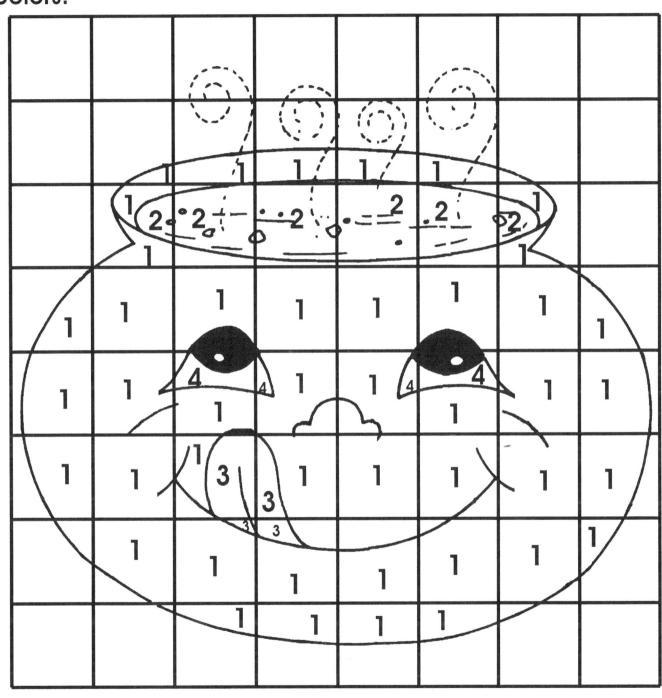

Color the 1's blue.
Color the 2's yellow.
Color the 3's red.
Leave the 4's white.

#298 Literature Activities for Young Children

Chicken Soup with Rice

September

a line connecting the numbers from 1-20. Color.

October

, , the pictures where they belong.

witch	goblin	ghost

November

Read the sentences below. ✏️ the spaces the correct colors.

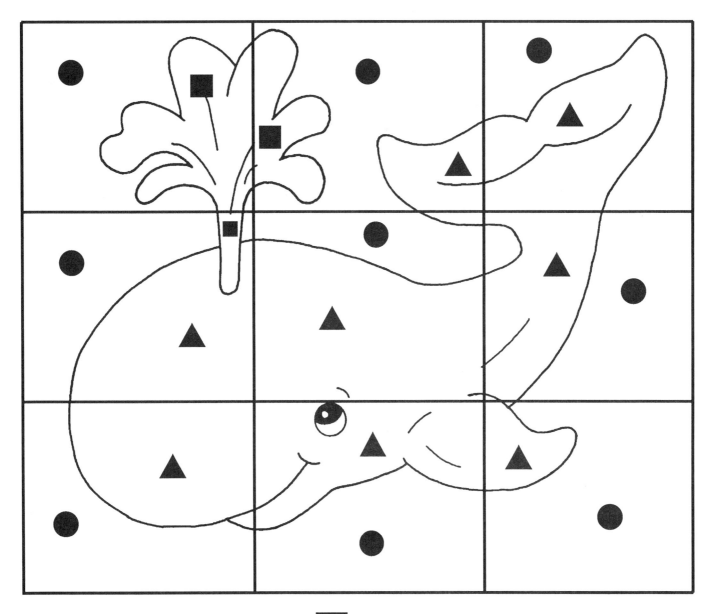

■ = green

▲ = gray

● = blue

December

the picture.   the words.

How many bowls are on the tree?

Christmas tree

Name_____

Chicken Soup With Rice

1. Color and cut out the pieces on pages 82 and 83.

2. Glue the pieces to a paper lunch bag (see diagram, below).

diagram

Chicken Soup With Rice (cont.)

The Land of Counterpane

a line from the whole to the part. Color.

My Shadow

Match the child to the correct shadow.

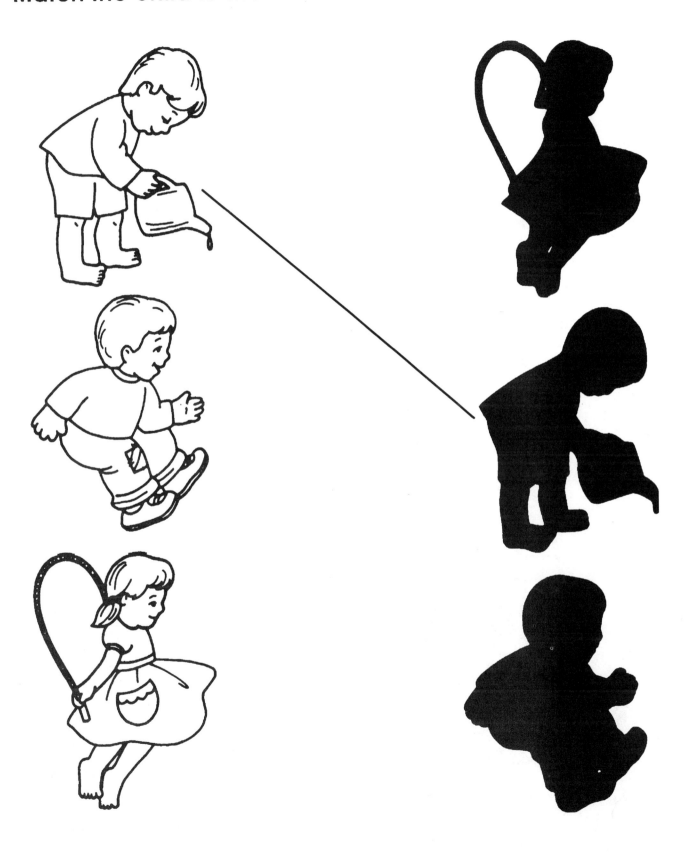

Marching Song

1. Color and cut out the pieces on pages 86 and 87.

2. Punch out holes A-D.

3. With string, attach the pieces to a coat hanger (see diagram at left).

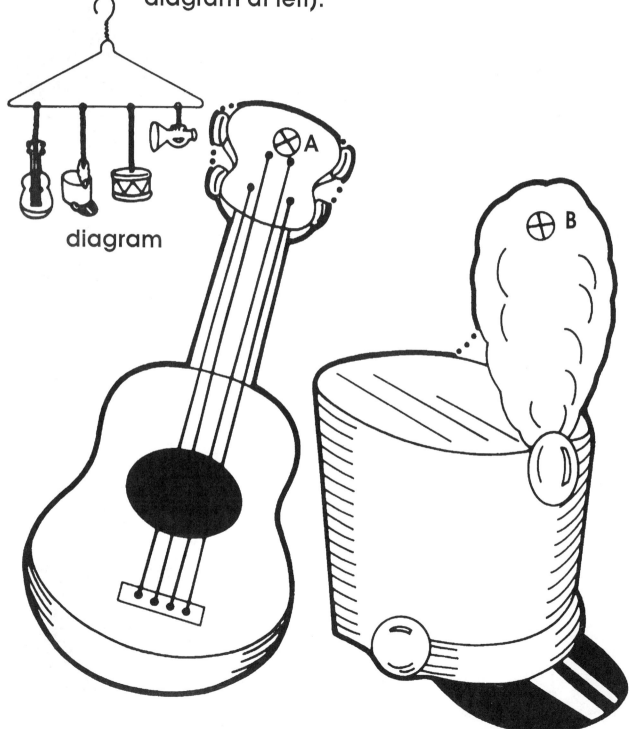

diagram

Marching Song *(cont.)*

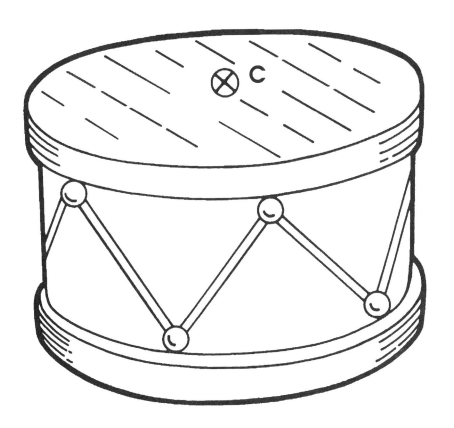

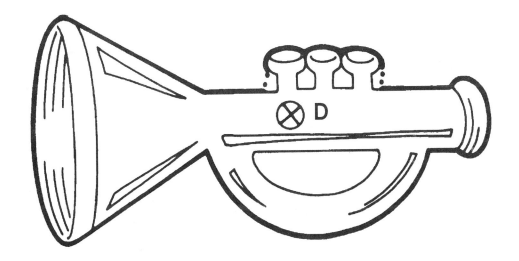

Name _____

The Cow

 and  the pieces onto construction paper to make a cow picture.

Happy Thought

 , ,   the pictures in the correct group.

people	animals
plants	**fish**

The Swing

1. Color pages 90 and 91.

2. Cut out the pieces below and glue them on top of the tabs on page 91.

3. Bend at dashed lines and open.

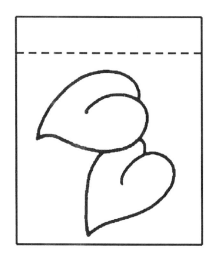

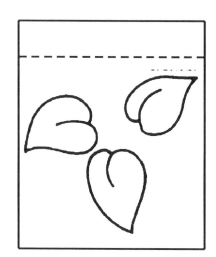

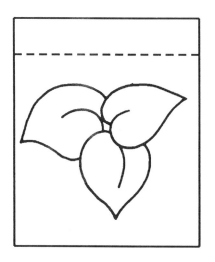

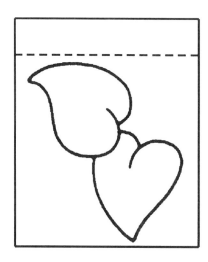

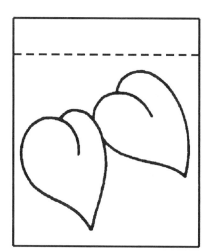

Name_____

The Swing *(cont.)*

Tab A

Tab B

Tab C

Tab D

Tab E

Tab F

My Treasures

1. Color and cut out the pieces on pages 92 and 93.

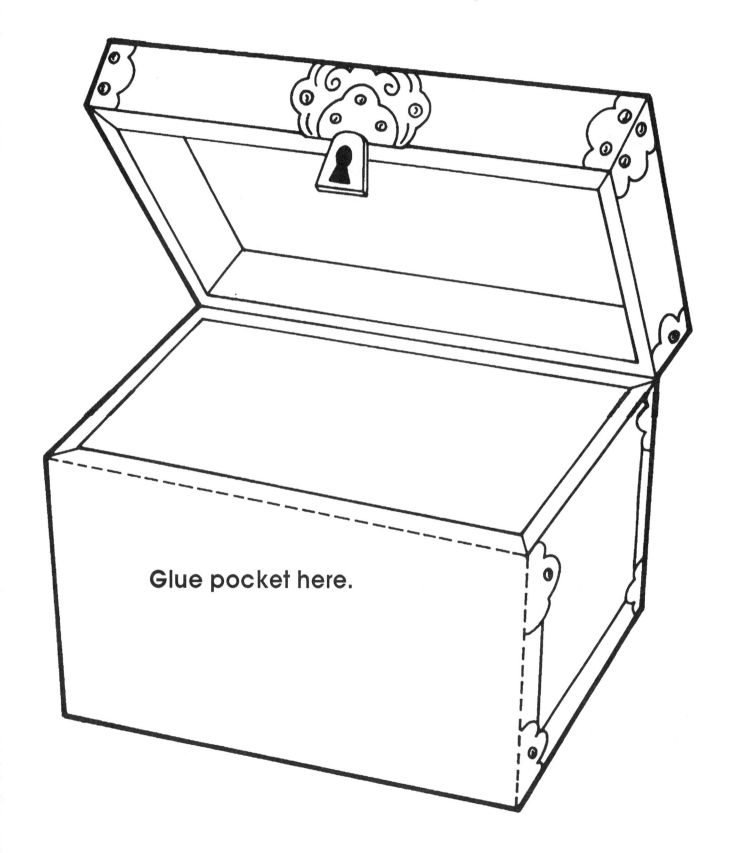

Glue pocket here.

My Treasures *(cont.)*

2. Glue the pocket, below, onto the bottom of the chest. Glue around the bottom and side edges of the pocket only, leaving the top open.

3. Put the cards in the chest in correct story order.

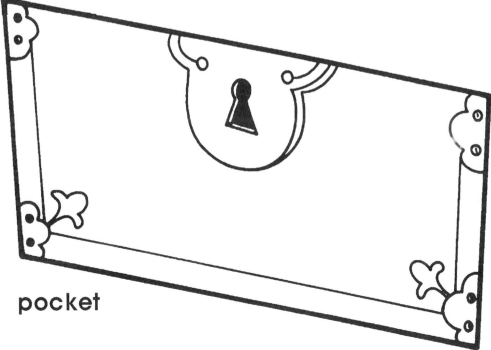

pocket

Block City

, , the pictures in order.

1	2
3	4

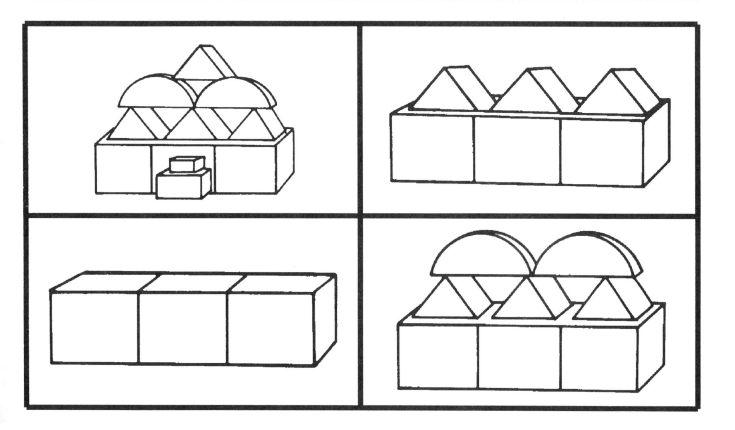

Nest Eggs

1. Color and cut out the pieces on pages 95 and 96.

2. Glue mother bird onto the nest (Tab A).

3. Glue the baby birds onto the nest (see diagram).

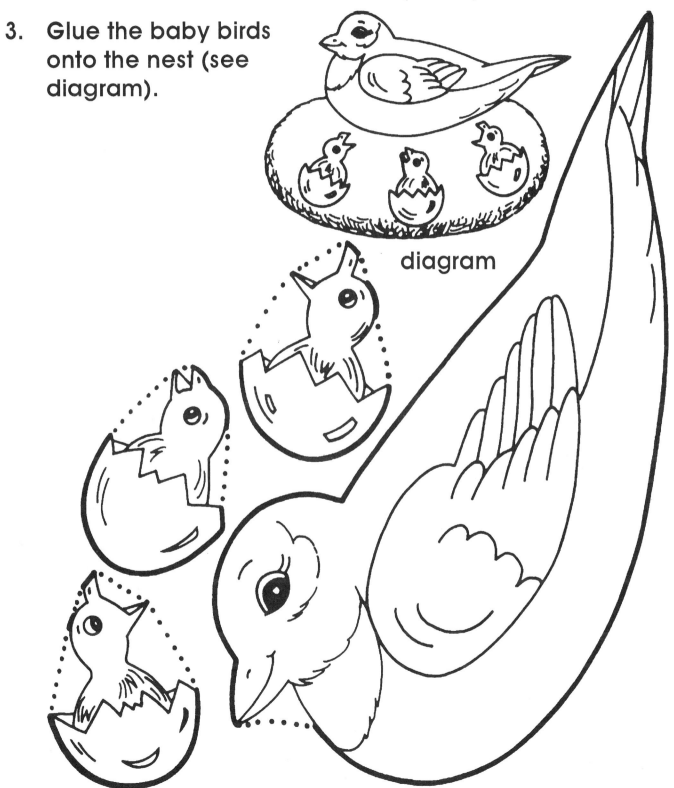

diagram

Nest Eggs *(cont.)*

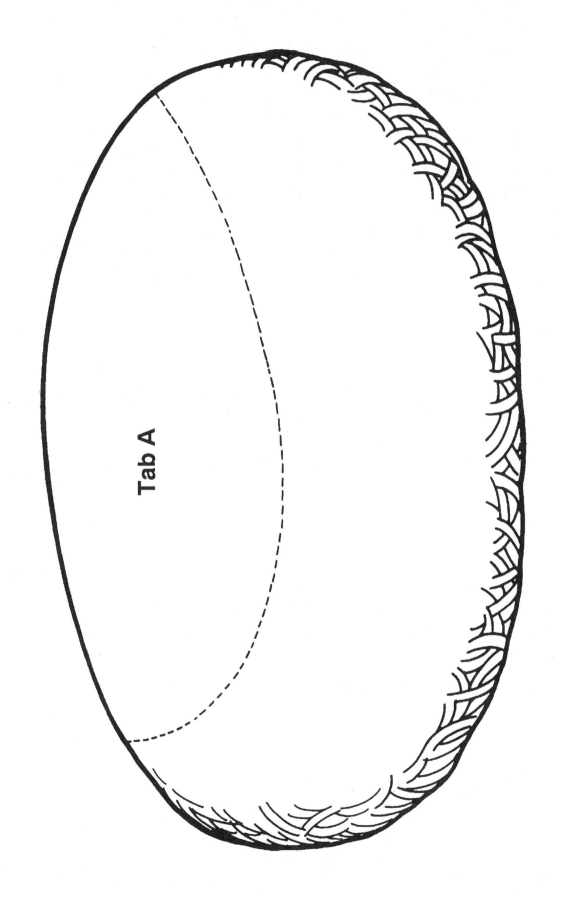

Tab A